Foxstruck
and Other Collisions

By the same author

The Non-Sequitur of Snow, 2015

Foxstruck
and Other Collisions

Shari Kocher

PUNCHER & WATTMANN

© Shari Kocher 2020
Cover image © Kate van der Drift

This book is copyright. Apart from any fair dealing for the purposes of study and research, criticism, review or as otherwise permitted under the Copyright Act, no part may be reproduced by any process without written permission. Inquiries should be made to the publisher.

First published in 2020
Published by Puncher and Wattmann
PO Box 279
Waratah NSW 2298

http://www.puncherandwattmann.com
puncherandwattmann@bigpond.com

A catalogue entry for this book is available from the National Library of Australia.

ISBN   9781925780789

Cover design by Miranda Douglas
Typesetting by Morgan Arnett
Printed by Lightning Source International

Contents

LEAD

All the Silver Ships You Carry	17
Foxstruck	19
Not the Horses	21
Mother Figures	22
White Desert Woman Sings to her Chickadees	24
Absent Self Portrait	26
Fritter the Fat Then Fry It	31
Black Door with Snow	35

TIN

In the Rothko Room at the Tate	39
Goats Cheese with Honey and Rosemary on Toast on a Sunday Morning	41
Peak-to-Peak Amplitude is also the sound of the wind on the tundra, singing	42
Errancy: a Primer	44
The Girl in the Mirror	46
Ode to the Crazy Road In and Out of Cycad Valley	48
As We Spiral Pine Tree Mountain	50
Ode to Considering the Lilies	51
Ode to Lutes and Ladders	52

IRON

Ode to difficult things   55
Vortex   57
Ode to Green   65
The Glimpse   67
Ode to Split Seconds from Marrakech   68
Ode to Immensity   69
Ode to the Upside-Down Oasis Within   71
Ode to the Erg Chebbi Dunes   72
Ode to My Father's Feet   76

GOLD

Forty Desert Days and Nights in White   81

COPPER

Implosion   91
Ode to Sludge   93
Keep going   95
Trespassers Beware of Snakes   96
Ode to the Not-I   98
Break, / 'the silent life-giver of worlds'   100
Ode to Earth   102
Notes on a Sunday night before sleeping   104

SILVER

Alphabet Unskinned: a Reader 109

MERCURY

Cusp 119
Wings 120
Bread 122
Sappho 124
Lacuna 126
Tidal 128
One 129
Breath 130
Questions 132

Notes 135
Acknowledgements 141

As if all there were, were fireflies
and from them you could infer the meadow.
—Rebecca Elson

Grief makes the heart
apparent as much as sudden happiness can.
—Jack Gilbert

We must continue to open in the face of tremendous opposition.
No one is encouraging us to open and still we must peel away the layers of the heart.
—Chogyam Trungpa

Perhaps someone else knows more, but not I.
—C.G. Jung

the one with violets in her lap
] mostly
] goes astray
—Sappho, fr. 21

I want to write pure movement.
—Clarice Lispector

*I saw a deer in a shaded wood
and knew that it was I who stood
between the lightning and the hollow tree
beating like a pulse in me.*

*Luminous creature with the fathomless eyes,
lines of grace without disguise,
a milk-mouthed fawn by her side,
drawn to the edge of the woods.*

*Drawn to the edge of the woods,
trembling there at the edge I stood,
salt on my lips, water on stone,
I and the deer and the milk-mouthed fawn.*

*Trembling, we return this night
to stand awhile in the vertical light
after the storm, fields of rain
quivering now, and now again.*

for Andi

LEAD

All the Silver Ships You Carry
an encaustic poem after Amy Melchior's encaustic paintings in *All the Silver Ships You Carry* (2018), and after Clarice Lispector's *A Breath of Life* (1979/2012) and Carson McCullers' *The Heart is a Lonely Hunter* (1940)

Cry Bird,
prey iridescent and restless,
kiss somebody's life.
I'm satisfied with being. Are you?
Smile.
Nothing
today wires zero complacently.
I tap into
this vital round without beginning.
I am the point before the zero.
From zero to infinity I walk
without stopping.
The day runs
along outside and abysses silence
me.
Miniature human,
valour of fluid passage,
those who labour and those who love
but for a moment only. Warning
shaft between the two.
Countered by glass, sweat
temples open wider
the delve more narrow
affrighted into a future blackness
error, ruin.
Between radiance and darkness, faith
sharply again no answer.
But *motherogod* could this terror
throttle like a jittery ninny

wet handkerchief beneath the water
tap somehow
the awning raised. Walk
inside. Soberly
the morning sun.
Milkwood. Oboe. Dark river
throated in widening circles.
Sunlight on seafoam.
Pink weed and leather kelp, jettied distraction.
The sun setting in the wrong direction,
the beach *I want* in full shade.
All this inscrutable
to write pure movement
smelted plankton, whale-sculpted,
cry Bird full circle back to
bay, bay, bay.

Foxstruck

Dinner done, dishes draining, the fire
a red glow in its dark box, I step tonight
beyond the porch light into grass
stiff with frost in the home paddock,
the night sky shelved but for the bright paw
and nose of the Dog Star chasing a hare
in the scudding dark, the almost
forgotten name of a flagship tossing
into view in a time before typhoid,
cholera and sweetened damper, the gorge
rising in the dip where shots rang out
last night, our feral neighbour licensed to
kill anything that moves, floodlit
and whooping just beyond our fence line
which a deer can clear in a moment if only
she knew she'd be safe here. But what's a fence
in a forest of stars? The cold eats fingertips
and ankles. If I had flares, I would light them.
Makes no sense how we got here. Makes
perfect sense: a fox, eye-locked, almost
touching me. Three red paws on the ground,
one white, lifted in mid-step, a thousand
tiny hairs sparking moonlight. Breath
a small vapour, electric. Eyes
like river stones, that old language
of fire held high in the brush-stroked tail
that pulses three feet of charged ground
sunk without sound in a heartbeat.
Foxstruck. Mist made mystic
at knee-height. Standing alone in a paddock
pouring electricity under a night sky

blinking cold atoms without answer,
blood quickens the slow burn of fox,
tricky as history, the fire before and after.

Not the Horses

not the horses, but their heartbeats.
not the houses, but the stumps.
not the river, but the damming.
not the fire, but the coal.
not the roaring, but the train track.
not the oat grass, but the ground.
not the boats, but the breathing.
not the mountain, but the sound.
not the pickets, but the shrieking.
not the factories, but the foal.
not the cattle, but the stungun.
not the fences, but the mud.
not the horses, but their heartbeats.
not the footprints, but the blood.

Mother Figures

There's one in the kitchen, all the food
tidied away, nothing to eat. All the chrome
gleaming. The tea-towels folded into eighths.
There's another at her sewing machine, her split
heels and one horned foot at the pedal
going hell for leather, mouth full of pins.

There's one in the laundry at the aged-care facility,
the ghost of her own mother steaming the nuns'
linens, cassocks, capes. Another over there,
organist on an upright chair, Bach on a Sunday,
who does she think, washing day is Monday
and women shouldn't vote.

One slams doors when angry, another presses
lips in silence thick as spit. Both scour windows.
Wear colour-coded slips. One says *I can't* at every
new thing. One lives in shame, with sex a sin.
One rushes past in a crackling dress that zaps
with electricity and seeps, supressed.

There are others. Sisters of these mothers.
And their mothers. One wore trousers
and choked on a fishbone, or swallowed
pills, it was never clear which. And yet another,
ladylike with lipstick, smartly dressed
but pitied as her father's favourite, still left

her daughters with him when he came to baby-sit.
All were young, or in their early prime, when,
trapped inside the marriage-carriage rhyme,

they left their fathers' houses to become
the mothers I embrace and run from.
These lines I trace defeat me.

How touch the shapes we live? One says
*I fear what you want is hardly reasonable,
given how hard it is to give.* Another tries to
say, but can't, because she's dying, *Dammit!
Let go.   Accept.   Forgive.*
One holds a child in her lap and sings.

White Desert Woman Sings to her Chickadees

First night in the dug-out
and I'm sitting up here on the roof
of her house, watching the sun
crash down in a three-sixty shower,
when out steps Ms. Spinifex in slippers,
jeans, cardigan. Shaded by trellis
and lopsided tin, she can't see me, but
I can see in the flare of her match,
the lift of her chin, the end of the day
breathing out and in, the biblical way
she tosses grain to her hens, the chirrup
and cluck of her half-dozen flock, red
as the cacti she tends with a can, red
the geraniums in crimson pots, red
as the dust on her pea-speckled flock,
the plume that wreathes each leathery foot,
the seeds they peck as she starts to sing
(in the hushed pink stillness of the windmill
grown still) serrated and dry
as this Spinifex hill, the hour of dusk
like smoke on a corner, the shimmering
splint of her fine-needled song, thin
in a throat grown silica strong with just
a hint of tumbleweed, fly-blown
rust—*Thirty-three years too late*, she sings,
three leathery eggs veined in red jammed
on a plate next morning—*Not from these parts*,
she says, as she switches the air-con off,
then on, and shivers underground in a white-
washed room amongst the rustling cups,
telling me how, in quick short puffs,

she'll be moving on, and coughs,
Moving on someday sometime soon.

Absent Self Portrait

 # white noise

              once a child is held
              by her father
              over a waterfall
              and told
              he will drop her
              if she doesn't stop
              crying
              upon a time is how
              a child learns
              what power is
              the noise of it
              she cannot stop
              even though she knows
              it's the open mouthed
              blowhole
              he cannot stand
              the waterfall tearing into
              that great white whale
              swimming through the hole
              in the path behind him
              she slips upon
              the name for it
              dangerous in her wet thongs
              halfway up or down
              the mossy stairs
              of that endless
              bush stalk to nowhere
              she cannot hear
              herself above the roar

so frightening but already
so much more
beautiful than she
has words for
waterfall
waterfall
the power of that pouring
loud inside her
even as she grows
exceptionally careful
about who she cries for
and how even now

"Mama, I'm as thirsty as a wall"

like the wobble on a bicycle with the bent spokes shining
like the clown folded forward with her bent bowler hat
like my grandmother's toenails turned brittle and black
like the cat bouncing backwards out of a cactus
like the deer bounding forward missing the car
like learning to walk again
like singing
like telling what happened before you were born
like giving birth in a dream twenty years later
like the static of storm clouds not quite gathering
like the tree on the corner split by lightning
like the tomb rolled open like trout returning
like the fur and sweetness of an overripe kiwi
like the smell of my mother's unopened chocolates
like the sting of her hairbrush thirty years later
like living to a hundred or halfway to eighty

       like the rust on the bicycle you loved as a child
       like the streamers though faded still streaming

salt

to dive into kelp clear as clouds is to swim ever closer to the razor fish rooted six feet deep shimmering twice their size & close enough to touch but falling away already peeling off her wetsuit in an upward rush the ozone hitting her shins with a sting that starts the fine invisible salt whips spindrift swaying into red so turning one foot on a chair my friend's step-mother swabs the cuts in iodine & her husband walking past sidesteps the question under his moustache & says *Aha! I see you've found your land legs!* & his wife with the red mouth laughs but with a hiss in her teeth & scolds me for not standing still enough & how the cuts sting like crazy the handle of the fruit knife spinning the plate with its pearly sheen like milk dipping the fish flesh balls in batter in a bowl on the bench where the fruit is piled high on a plate in the corner & squeezing sticky as laughter from wrist to elbow the juice of lemons my fourteen-year-old friend & I (not) crying (not ever) crying in company *she's got guts that one* the hiss of gas flickering blue under his hands as the fish begin to fry her lower limbs laced in red & irresistible two dogs under the table waiting for chips who lick & lick & lick

'The desert has many teachings'

       Turn towards emptiness, the mountain said.
       And there she was every morning,
       blue turning purple turning pink.

       My empty mountain, the one
       I could not climb. Every night
       my bed on the ground grew

softer, I did nothing to change it.
Every night I dreamt of water.
It just grew softer by itself.

Every morning I woke in tears.
Turn towards emptiness, she said.
And I did.

She was the one crying through me.
Every time she came to wipe my eyes
I grew lighter, I grew light.

kite strings, New Mexico

So I left my portrait in the vault
on purpose, not wishing to fold it
or roll it between six cities, the seventh
being this desert I return to
                with more than I can carry,
                yet the portrait I made in the
                presence of others in a room
                full of bees in a thunderstorm
is not where I left it, is
nowhere. I ask Evelyn, since
she has the key and seems
partly luminous, returning
                like the moon, empty handed.
                I'm sorry, she says, her smile
                so cheerful I smile into the eyes
                of a goddess who tells me

the vault, for some reason, is empty.
Between us, there spins
the ghostly grin of something
mislaid in the bowels of this place
            that used to belong to the witches.
            Who knows what has become
            of that riot of animals and wild
            interiors and colour so glorious
it hurt in a good way to look at it?
Perhaps the trance it was made in
has gifted it back, and all my Invisibles
are walking with bits of my portrait
            strapped to their hearts
            and attached to their heads, seven
            threads to the land of the butterfly
            pulling my absence on kite strings.

Fritter the Fat Then Fry It

Narrator:

    Once upon a time a house
    all the modcons. etcetera but she flits

    vagrant as a dandelion's flimsy puff
    blowing about in a yard

    empty of air and light a hole
    shucked to the floor like a skin

    all that space shut-up
    the chimney sealed

    against birds
    smoke and one

    homeless soul
    chewing her finger

    nail outside the door slipped
    sideways into maternity

    ward of the state where once she laboured
    abandoned to her fate under the weight

    of sixteen generations of women
    who lived to be fed to the dogs

    day after day without complaint.
    Perfecting the Art of Self-Restraint.

Ah well, enough of that. Here comes
the corpse with the luminous eyes

abandoning all art and artifice
in loving this woman who labours against

these shut-up rooms
this keep-out fence

come to bid her soul to rise
come to claim her house.

Corpse and Narrator speaking to Belovèd:

Rise cheese, rise mouse.
Rise gently, fair house.

Take this!
    cries the corpse, throwing open the door.
Take this,
    she pants as blood floods the floor.

Here is a fire, a kettle, a fish.
Sweep open the chimney—what is your wish?

Tearing, she screams and the sound bounces back.
Scream! says the corpse and clenches her fists.

Tell me, Belovèd,
   what is your wish?

Belovèd's voice overlayed by Narrator and Corpse:

      The thing is, it's not the children
who want to eat you
though they cling with their many mouths
stabbing and pulling at you
always hungry: that is their right.

      Beware
when he says you can't
because of the children
because of the house
because of the job
because you wouldn't
because you are too kind …
The children are not the cause of your Mummy-hood.

      Wake up.
See that chair in the corner by the window?
See those jars with the animal heads?
I don't understand this darkness, you say, *repeated in waves
like dreaming.*
      Wake up.
*Jackal, falcon, baboon
the one with the human form …*
      Wake up.

Why, dismembered, do your feet keep walking?
Why praise unholy ground?
See the thickness of the light, see the burning?
You are the sacrifice. This is your pyre.

Wake up—Belovèd—the world's on fire!
Throw off your bindings, tinder tight!
Children, Children, the world's on fire!
Curse this linen—it blocks the light!

Quickly now—you must assemble
—rising from this bed—
the separate wires of our eyes
the severed static of your head.

Belovèd embraces Narrator and Corpse to produce a litter of verbs:

pummel the flood of beguile	bewilder me brave to sleep
swarm swath delve dwindle	undo constrain leap me
past your droning mob	slough off dullness wrestle tilt
torch the harass of cradle	thank the thrum now hold it
hoist the harvest ladle	funnel harrow weep
rejoice in sky yes tarnish	the tilt of loom and tangle
unravel it fathoms deep	lop off and lope to the forfeit of logic
the pine of ache in ashy water	be done with it make
the nearness and dearness of dwell	unfasten the harness infest
with wonder shine the raze	on dread limn this night
with lowering stars and oblong	doorways peeling pewter
plunder and spread	the delicate pinion of a butterfly's
wing poised on a snapdragon's	stamen here be here and sing it!
[all rise]	refuse to play dead

Black Door with Snow

after Georgia O'Keeffe: *Series 1 – From the Plains, 1919* and *Black Door with Snow, 1955*

> *The essential thing is what we always miss.*
> —Jorge Luis Borges

Warm billowing swill of night, I hold you back, I pull you tight.
This will not do. It's not alright. I hate the rhyming
pangs of night. The frankfurters shrivel in their pink skins.
The pot, boiling over, sizzles dry and when you call,
petroleum singes greygreen coffee eyes.
Black Door with Snow, I'd rather leave you open
but Dot once said of Death (misquote) *you're not simple
and neither am I*. I
refuse to believe (but reserve the right for later) O
damn it, I will not cry. How come blue lightning strung
with Buddha's tears swarms in kernels, lime *Sturm und Drang*
the second time, a second call, another round of rind? *He'd better
fast track those handyman jobs and paint the downspout green,
or I'll be stuck with it*, my mother says. And then, there's the other,
a shadow on her lung, a ball of liver, two more hairy balls
sprouting in her brain, and my father with his tarmac tincture,
nothing lost, nothing gained. *Nothing is still something*,
absence says, and then the phone flaps dead, not
for want of coins or payment plans or my father's steely
Bring on the drugs, I'm not complaining. Tensile
the drill of satellites ahead, herding dis-comfortable sheep.
Night with its brush of mushroom accordions.
Stars stuck on with lipstick, finger paint and sleep.

TIN

In the Rothko Room at the Tate

Through the pink funereal door
the smudged lit crack is more
than light   *Calor*   the grey absconding
night   whose twin-striped suit-set

speaks *Father* on his way out
to have a smoke with death or
what about desire   but the bars
are twin prisons he can't rewrite

and the backwash of the pillar   red
the hinge a depth   so slight
no revolving door this backward glance
unframed   rectangular flight   no

calming wall   *nothing* nothing
a knife   I   might
the furnace edged in fire   shadow
pink discharge a turning

blueblack tongue   in thickness numb
square rings that flare   the whole
in verbs   made dull
withholding   a   glow

only shadows mauve
the bruise unholy   Light on oily
water   a whiff of drains
and angels   squeeze

a lily inside an egg   pulse pink
   shifting   liminal
         mundane
fever   & fairy bread

bent ribbons   blackboards
the breath and body of whence   I

Goats Cheese with Honey and Rosemary on Toast on a Sunday Morning
after Gaston Bachelard's *The Psychoanalysis of Fire* (1964)

Fire having made us, heat becomes us.
Hands that milked the goat and bee,
the bee that milked the flower, equally
your hands, last night and this morning
churn, to set, to rise, to spread
this yeast in me the fire alights
along the rosemary sprig; to savour

the passing of hands through love
is what we swallow in this space
coming together and apart: fire
the food of medieval thought, our
exhalations feeding comets, yes,
our breath the stuff of stars. Be
careful with those gum leaves so near

the kindling box: just like the classic laurel
brushed, so too my heart, when shaken,
sparks, and *that which has been licked
by fire has a different taste,* fragile
as this earthly grace, which burns the sun
behind your head and turns the little blue
flowers red *as do the bones of lions.*

Peak-to-Peak Amplitude is also the sound of the wind on the tundra, singing
after Rebecca Elson

Lions pollinate our dreams with ultraviolet,
or do they? Picking their way lightly
over your dreaming body to nest in belly
nook and back, the skirling in the
understorey, three yellow pears, a plume
of pine scent, all the frost-clad grasses

and shivering flats. In the quantum
quickening, in darkness, a buoyancy
barely remembered, all at once,
whatever you have forgotten to imagine
sweeps light through cells to call
your soul entire, whoever

you are, centuries perhaps in the
parting, a living perfume not yet born
of whom I kiss the inner palms,
and the paws: a planet who can dream
like this and let touch the outer
mountain, and move it. The rapid

crystal, the languid pools,
the spruce and granite and alder
asparkle with the lightest of wave
functions, each lit particle even more
deliquescent than the flake caught
on velvet and magnified. To you,

I send out a lantern in the snow,
a blue and red tipped tundra swan at
dusk, dew in the morning running on
bare feet to meet you, running
to sweep you into—precisely this.
Can twin flames exist?

So be it. Dark matter
distilled, delicate as a
dandelion's simple flower,
the exact geometry of the flake
that fed the seed and became it,
when buried under snow.

Errancy: a Primer
after Emily Dickison

one spinning sunflower

so I fall through the heart	of a sunflower standing tall
in a too small plot	a blue picket fence
the blue-black	bristle-tipped rush of my
falling the pith and burn	darkness lit in geodesics
the brine of midday	made crystal by nightfall
your sweet revolving	eclipse of granite
on tawny moss	a dolomite spark
held out in laughter	ally of touch the summit
a sunflower shower	kernels magnetic
before the beginning	and after

two woollen socks

into whose laps all good things fall	I know too much too well
numinous inside the real	in fantasy to dwell is but
another way of walking into	the ocean through
partitioned rooms	a fondness for forgotten things
enschrined by early service	the daily devotion
no less difficult in practice	my heart in darkness is also
a green and brimming fountain	the purl of knitted socks
habitual kindness	undone by dust
storms of discontent	and forgiveness
we were young once	children between us
our feet wrapped in felted pelts	still the fibres that bind us

three singing hearthstones

in radiance the sting	in dimness gloaming
in him I am a rainbow	in her a silver fish
a single water droplet	held in finest mesh
dewlapped in extremity	joy the radius of blue
flying rounded corners	wide the wide-eyed darkness
the tinder in the bulb	mountain ash and sassafras
imprinting fossil faces	rime on crescent fringe
violet in dissolve	swept by a crinkling sea
aerial self unspoken	a river in every tree

five pointed clocks

in simple rings	grown three score ten
time divides the infinite	flight into seasons
thick and thin	shivers the wind
floats fury	joy and sorrow
seared in fire	yesterday tomorrow
poplar pine river oak	olive grove and briar
narrow girth whose birth	cut into clocks
teeth spit	air and rain
wires	set before
eternity	a tick inside the brain

The Girl in the Mirror

for Joan Fleming

at sixteen
the girl in the mirror
alone with her shadow
in a house full of crazies
for a week by the sea

the shape of that stone
alone for a week without
going crazy
in a shadowy houseful
of time by the sea

tenacious and strange
just her and me the touch
of her kindness shim-
flicker true the size
of that stone and the sea-

sound of her gentling
mind on me each plate
washed as if to placate
the place I'd become (from)
the shower wiped free

just sketch she said just
sketch what you see
the grain of the wood
on the windy deck the scab
on the knob of your knee

nothing is ugly she
said just sketch and see
the knife that cuts can
turn to stone and stones
can roll like sea-

weed blown from kelp to
curtains shim flicker sewn
at sixteen she smiled there is
much to see in a shadowy
house full of time by the sea

Ode to the Crazy Road In and Out of Cycad Valley

                        young rock
                        old rock
                        Lizard Rock rocking
                        where rock touches air

touched by water
carved and holding
faces in the rock
all dancing
                        the no-go road
                        better try walking
                        or kangaroo jumping
                        see that one old man

watching sun country
that one young woman
with sleepy eyes
nah only joking
                        you're one crazy white
                        woman look I can disappear
                        faster with the car
                        doors locked

no water what you
thirsty? there's a yoni
squiggled in rock
see that spider's saliva
                        you better not come
                        looking for me sun
                        baking there's a dancer
                        in profile dancing there's a

swarm of hate this
whitefella crazy energy
sinkhole dead place
watcha make me come for?
                          sleepy lizard that one
                          whole head rocking
                          the trees are talking alright
                          full of tree talk today
there's a hand cupped
another one pointing
there's a palm shivering
a palm to the ground

As We Spiral Pine Tree Mountain

What small herbs of ice and wind
are carried, glinting, seven spirals
through a ring, this skin-tingling
shiver-flickering ruckus of imported
scent upon us, this space between

our bodies and our shadows
soft-footed in needles three feet deep?
I confess I've watched you turn,
out walking, to check how far behind
I've fallen, and if too much, fling

yourself to ground, coming home to this,
this here, home country, despite the foreign
trees, whose roots are tangled like yours
in mine, dropping down beside you
in full sweat, the bed of your smile

so worth it, out of breath, that I could lie
here forever pouring the mountain
through the pine, not once, but many times
these past weeks following the Bogong moth
and this—this untranslatable rush

of heat sparked by your hand in mine
which shoots the bird in me straight
up through the roar of history, that trap-
door floor a canopy unhinging
the sky in us as we fall and fall

and rise in flood as sap inside a tree.

Ode to Considering the Lilies

Where lilies flame the gravel path
Love falls away to flower into
what if, what if   there Sleep pours her
water nets through a stream that lifts

so nebulous it can't be seen except
where Spring meets sky   and *what if*
brings   all it touches to
emptiness   through the flaming

hand that reaches   and is met
while one foot burns the gravel
path and the other   almost flesh
flenses the flame tree   and pours

ten   thousand
sulphur crested cockatoos
wheeling through   forever
at the lip   as when hands

touch tenderness lit   the flaming
lilies do not burn   but flare

Ode to Lutes and Ladders
after Hagit Grossman

In the lives I live at night while dreaming, always a house on a cliff with a blue door set inside

a white wall containing a hundred other houses with blue doors and white walls filled with music and lilacs, carpenters and dancers, whose voices punctuate the stillness and carry across

the sea. In this night poem, you are the Friend who throws down the key, who sets the candles in pyramid cloves, and I am the Other who enters, inhaling the scent of oranges and honeyed pistachio bells, glad I haven't had to cook, and twirling, glad to greet our friend the Raven who

has just dropped by with a newly written song and a kitten he begs a dish of milk for. Upstairs, children travel in their beds, the children of your children, and even your lover's children, and someone is playing a lute on the rooftop next door, while the moths pour in and out the open window and a longed-for lacy curtain sweeps the tender floor. Always a little music

blowing in from somewhere. Like the stranger who arrives bearing a silver fish wrapped in newspaper, which your husband takes to cook in a fusion of lemon and thyme. Soon a midnight feast is going on as you lick your fingers and listen to the one who sings and plays her most mysterious and newly written song. Nights like this are not so rare, but still the rarity awakens something in us to do with lutes and ladders and easy friendship and not one of us is sleepy yet

there are plenty of cushions and the moths drift in and out like curtains and the candles burn quietly down.

IRON

Ode to difficult things

The green growl of fur in the cat's
belly a bellows
the folded mouse sleeps upon,
her tail wrapped round her

opened innards: the pickerel
light that deepens
in the beam held open:
the wild marrow a chasm

in orange upsweep, the
ground heat
pouring through a grated
weight of light:

her felted
mouse-ness unfolding
inside the hunched cat
who retches peaceably

the patient fur coughed upward
(slim, the yarrow's unfurling,
wide, the molecular drift—
as birds

chase smaller birds,
and even a fieldmouse,
into the darkness
(what splendour the fire-lit hall,

the chitter swept through
in a blink
so wildly brief and yet
so slim the touch that sweeps

the briefest mouse-bone
beyond the pink
nest of her squirming babies,
beyond the yellow rapeseed

(*heaven without rent or seam*
tangled and timeless and torn—

Vortex
after Jorie Graham

for Gayle de Angelis

#Fierceness

Actively resisting
the airport alarms going off in all directions, silence
bequeaths a sanctuary, the quiet
temples rinsing their radiance through
the Basho bell of every mechanical
flower. I am not going to argue
light on lightness and in darkness,

(a velvet lash radiating the rim)
such fierce and chosen softenings,
(certainly not *if only*) but given the choice,
seven textless circles in the sky moving eastward,
the steamship at the threshold
of yesterday's blinking, one wooden
board rotted right through, despite

the freshly painted moonlit railings,
the birds settling the night inside the fig
that knocks against this corner aerial
newly ghosted in orange lamplight—
I am not
a single Stop sign closing its eye
on the lap of the traffic lulling last night's

in-drawn breath, deep and fringed and open to
the sharp drop of ocean turning
blue dunes to foam to
those little isotopes of radiation
indrawn, exhaling
night after night into mourning—
I am not.

#*Sweetness*

Teacupped in conversation,
the wind galloping on the way to Gayle's,
steeped in waves pouring the hill over and over
without spilling a single drop, the tidal
grasses, the bay
tree flooded with finches, speckled
peewees, periwigs, lorikeets and grebes,
our conversation a full-blown banksia bowing under
phalanxes of uncorked buds, already dried and
hardening into cobs, into callows, into cones,

the yellow rue with its spidery lacework, the giant
poppies on their slender stalks turning back into
themselves, crimson frisked to naked bulbs, the rigid
star inside the centre of every poppy flower, o
electric blue, and dipped in ink, my heart
(a fabric printer's paradise) thickening
the poppies' green applehard cheeks, the bulbs
in rounded cat-among-the-pigeons ripening uncut
and dug into a flourishing feast of future flowers
waving their flounces on opium necks, the figs

unfurling their waist-high umbrellas, the purple
echinacea in hoarded hubs, windmills
of marigolds, borage and sage, the lemon tree
buried in blossoming bees, wave upon wave,
the walrus wind inside the kangaroo paws
whirling invisible castanets,
picking up sticks in the wind and stamping
my tangled heart westward, dipping under
hammock and birdbox, the hexagonal hum
growing louder the closer I come

to the beebox, the woodpile, the compost, the fence,
the beech trees softening their pixilated purr, the feather-
topped grasses conceding, dreamy among the miraculous
moss, where the wombat has snuffled and scraped through
the night, and the bobolinks and crickets are curling the pith
of the pouch-shaped patch I lay myself down in,
re-hearing rounded woodnotes of wind in yesteryear's slim
water rustled to wattled whisper, forest mulch and fungi
quickening beneath the dried beech blossoms
in their yellow cones, flicking past on wings.

#Wordlessness

Collecting clouds
in a basket, leaning into the substance time
does not dictate, smokeshapes
breathe a bristling

reed wall in woven skullcaps
whose surface-trembles, edged and edgy,
make quick effervescent circleshapes,
spears that dimple

the point at which each reed emerges,
sheathed inside a barely perceptible sac,
that trembling point of contact between
reed, water, air,

where a starling's fingerseed
flickering in branched shadow hops
sprinkles movement too quick
beneath the water forming

roundthrust silkskinned
tambourine rushes, small shivers
smoking outwards in rapid
sparks, the almost

submerged violin trembling
beneath the living sting,
a limpid skyglass
latent, hovering.

#*Fire*

Skin on skin,
the salted rose a flood, more
salt glistening on snow-swept blood,
bitter herbs enfolding
the bluest flower

pulsing half-moon blue,
a quantum leap, gold-shucked,
the sky-scratched eye at half-mast in lashes
closed and closing, instant blue
driftshapes, blissborn, rising

nine slow earth steps to the fledgling
pear tree, sitting cross-legged on buffalo grass,
the flatfur weeds fire-wedged acutely,
the pear trunk high as a thigh and turning
three wire threads, a metal stake, rust

the colour of an insect
going about its microbial business
caught in the flatfur granules which sting
when you rub them, finger to thumb,
skin sting, stung.

#Surrender

The honeycombed cliffs walk
the shallow rockpools wrinkling their unwrinkled rims,
where fingerlings dart across shoulders and the bone-

marrow light enters skin cells and soles, all the silver
ships you carry coming in and leaving
green surf cliffslaps in rising crescendos

the urge to say *yellow*, every grain on fire,
crystallised saltspray a symphony
of underwater wind

whose sunshapes cave
with gulls and squawking children
treading periwinkles and clams, a single fluted

seahorse, curved spine sleepshaping,
textless circles on the spot
coming to nest among rocks,

where a pink-suited child on her belly flaps
warm ecstasies of shallow water, hooks
mica, shell-grit, colourless

fault-lines to wind-fluted crumblings,
kelp pod, crab husk, black
lantern lumps mistaken for coal.

#*Solace*

Walking an ocean in the rain,
whose damp aromatics meet heat in motion,
the succulent pigface flowers
turn their Zion lips upwards in fleshy chortles,
holding back

a shivering poodle, who is intent on tugging at
the lead (*what leads beyond?! beyond?!*) this jagged
crush of cliff and foam, all the slicked grasses bent double
worshipping the roaring rocks, the doggy-licked ground,
o happy wet dirt sponged to fullness

drinking in the rain in crisp, round skysounds,
sharing a muffin at the kiosk with aforementioned poodle,
who vacuums up every last crumb, my muted
mood palette breaks thunderously open in three
sudden cloud pillars steaming westward

across a blazing carpark
across a footbridge with silver rails
across a frangipani road shaded by figs
across a tree-lined stillness dripping blue umbrellas
across a courtyard, a foyer, a cold cascade,

two glass-panelled slidings, almost invisible, crossing
carpet like quicksand and breathing
the anarchist whispers of plastic-bound books
on straight-jacketed shelves, unbuttoning a
perfectly provincial blue-buttoned chair,

the sesame-seeded cookery section giving off
the faintest whiff of mustard.

#Laughter

bubbles up out of the belly, big
buddha-bellied laughter bounces up
that inner gleaming
wide-hipped, big-breasted, fire-in-the-belly
singing in the shower, cooking up a storm,
the steam alive to the pure wet joy of it
without a single note of hearing coming
out wet and letting the wind dry
the beach this morning, air-whipped,

frustration stored in static feet
released in ludic merriment, the almost
unbearable breath of a dandelion
dancing roundly through
a kookaburra world and its impossible
landings, the lush and lucent layers of a dying
creek bed which sprouts weeping-rice grass,
kangaroo grass, blue-bellied bulb grass, one bent
blade already seeded into seven spear-shaped gutturals,

grassy soles that sigh in audible puncta,
stems as strong as wire sprung
to humming, two bent blades wringing
anti-alleluias: touched one way, a
coarse green-haired softness, touched
the other, and the blade bites:
ten thousand invisible teeth retaining water,
a brown-lipped quiver of heat in motion
balanced on the tip of every listening blade.

Ode to Green

Children are a necessary
evil, my mother says, and chokes
on a mango smoothie I have not
spun in the processor long enough.
Use them all, she'd said, thrusting
the frozen cubes at me from behind,
but the clip-locked bag is bulging
and there's no way I can get
all those mango bits to fit. Her choking
has a wheezing sound
like asthma. I run to fetch
a glass of water.
The drops glisten on the outside
of the water glass as I hand the end
of last summer to my mother, who has
rushed out onto the street and is choking
into her crossed arms, head bent over the kerb.
You forgot the ice-cubes, she rasps,
but takes the glass and returns to the porch
and sets it down on the chair
I have just leapt up from.
I resist the urge to run back inside to fetch some.
We resume
our salad of rocket, pear and parmesan.
The winter sun touches our hands and faces.
I probably have the same as he had,
she says. I grow still
and wait,
watching my mother purse her lips to take
the smallest of sips from her water glass.
I was emotionally deprived, too, you know.

It's not as easy as you think.
She stabs at the rocket on her plate.
Marjorie, for instance, won't eat anything green.
No wonder she's so fat.
I let the sun invade my skin cells.

The Glimpse

for Penny Drysdale

To open into the day-wide-day and find it wanting.
To go out anyway, no small thing.
To find, without looking, the whole day tossing

its largeness from limb to limb crying out *Look! Look!*
To walk into that light and its musical river,
to touch, in particles of wood and water, its

mysterious clamour, which overnight has stormed
a new rock pool that churns the infinite whirl
to quicksilver—that silent leap—a platypus

my human shadow casts its cold upon. To dive into
darkness—gone—the live wire of her wet surprise
a song—articulate, intelligent—the lucent gift

the day gives anyway—its merry swish
hauling me up and over—bone, flesh, breath tripping
at the speed of light through my spirit's sun gate.

Ode to Split Seconds from Marrakech

A skinned goat's head
at my elbow launches me
quickly but carefully over raw
puddles on slippery cobbles, the smell
of cat and camel piss alongside
the eating motions of the men
on the corner filling their mouths
with cupped fingers directed at three

young Western women walking
towards us—I glance away in steady
revulsion, downward, the uneven cobbles,
and up again to walnuts and oranges,
a pyramid of figs, pink
lettuce heads flowering in clay pots,
and a man lounging in a hooded robe
with camel feathers on his feet.

What to do with bamboo next to
a prickling cactus, a turquoise door,
the arch of palm trees in full sway,
rubbish-strewn, yes, but still the cliché
of palm shadow latticed against a lintel,
whose portal moves like water
over amber, coral, and Berber silver?

Knock-knock. The amulet touched
by sewage, rain and muted dust.

Ode to Immensity

My heart is a goat's bladder dizzy with strain.
Travelling East on a high road, cloud shadows rolling,
my heart is a wasteland of flowering almonds,
a verdant, mud-sluiced, rubbish-strewn ditch.

O break me and mend me and render me open.
I have never before, so wishing otherwise
Sweet earthlight
in softness, in blue light and grit.

Mapless and mazed and mindless, asunder,
flinching at plastic in mud rushed red,
I trail and fail to name you, *Ouarzazate*,
tasting the chaos of this hard-boned bed.

I am that slope-shouldered dog, and also that perky one.
I am that sleepy dog, and also that working one.
I am the horn of this bus
and the swerve of a pick-up truck

brushed left and right, bewildered by sight,
lone dog in traffic who pivots and freezes
and I—I meet the eye of the on-coming driver,
who burns through us both, does not flinch

and does not stop. Soft burst of impact,
my bowels are opening this Ode in my notebook
turning to slush—what happens to a soul
whose life meets indifference? What dies

in this world for the dog on the road?
What happens to the three weather-worn
faces in the tray of the pick-up truck
enduring our photographs?

My heart is a wasteland of olives in rows.

My heart is a donkey asleep on its feet.
A three-walled river-house returning to mud.
A cracked yellow pot containing a cactus.
A rubber-leafed succulent, knocking.

My heart is a boy on a fountain wall
in a violin square playing under his chin
yesterday's donkey in a valley of roses
tethered to a stake in the burning wind.

The walls of Kelaat glow orange at sunset.
They gather unto themselves a late-petalled rose.

Ode to the Upside-Down Oasis Within

Heedless, I dive headfirst into the well
at dawn, the water still holding the faded
faces of stars. Here I come to the underside
of the prickle-barked oasis tree, here

I come to the upside-down Oasis within.
Call it an inverted dome, a Spring.

There's a rustle in the reeds and Sekhmet
laps with her lion's tongue ripples that
enter the soles of my feet like incense.
Flat under moonlight, floating dunes

in the sky, names do not die but sail
toward us, the body
a many-chambered echo of fiery
star folk warming the cells

within. Light
as diaphanous cloth on skin
night hands creased with oil
and saffron: *Begin*.

Wordless, I am given to know
I never want to leave this place. I go.

Ode to the Erg Chebbi Dunes

I

Camelprints
in kidney shapes
flute us forward—

distance
is chalk,
and blows

II

a spheroid of desert sparrows
and one large black
crow, unceasing.

III

Sandstorm herds us
close-packed like so many white
oversized sheep.

Face-flayed
from tent to kitchen,
the Berber oven

a mud bricked
furnace of darkness
and heat.

Hoary camel tent flap.
Rock-freighted blanket.
Knees touching.

Where on earth.
None of us
can sleep.

IV

Where does the wind house itself when it's not blowing?
Where does it go between puffs? Call it
a bark house, a house made of blankets, a palace
of clouds east of the sun—who welcomes the wind
going homeward? Who runs

vertical hand-strokes down rippling walls,
sand shirring like smoke on the ridges?
Three palm trees, and Karen's
excellent blanket held up by sticks
make a sweet place in shade for our rest stop,

but now we are windborne, windlathed, faceflensed
and all the countless bits of grit are getting into everything.

Houseless, the wind winds me up,
even as it unwalls us.

V

Swung by the knees
on a razor ridge,
letting go

car trips on family
holidays, backseat
nausea unvoiced,

warblers in the palm
thickets watering
our camels' sideways

tongues in reefs
made of sandstorm,
and the music just after

time hangs
loose as a palm frond,
and rows

VI

shadows larger than origins
in light
choreographies of wind.

A footprint, mine.
A lodestone, white.
My back to the bone-box.
My head on my knees.

I am thinking about the thinnest of ground crusts, with little cracks in it.
I am thinking about the tenacity of weeds.
If I am honest, I am also thinking about fig jam, pillars, and toilets,
the absence of porridge and the distance from home.

Your dear worried face and receding hairline; your wrists and your delicate bones.

How, though you're sleeping, your bees are still humming,
your new dream of boxes and freshly cut wood,
your twine measured out between stakes and an apple press,
your rocks laid in circles; my face turned away.

Seven cairns make an apple tree in seated formation.
Clouds, cast in bird hops, click faces of stone.

Already the shadows lie smaller than origins.
Already the sharpness of bone.

Braham's axe in the distance twice echoed in wood.

A footprint, mine.
A lodestone, white.
My back to the bone-box.
My head on my knees.

Ode to My Father's Feet

South of my heart
unalloyed, adamantine
my father's feet
swollen like water balloons
turning to gourds as large as knees
watermelon soft, vermillion

and the bottle, upended, spills over
his feet propped up
propped huge and flowering
on one of my mother's
green towel-covered footstools
and my father says yes to the rose oil

my father says yes to the rose oil
arranging the towel that has slipped
and my mother cuts open
the legs of his trousers
as none with the swelling will fit
and my father says yes to the rose oil

his feet in lumpen lodestones
nails curled mothish and black
my father says yes to the rose oil
his jellyfish toes aflock
floating purplish grapes
ay, south of my heart

a prayer cut short mid-strut
O let me feast my eyes
upon your Skyclad body

the red and pink cloth
the women of Nimro
billow forth in clouds of dust
driving the hard road into the desert
from the back of a cart shrouded in black
my father says yes to the rose oil

south of my heart
the wind-winnowed walls waver on ledges
where three bent figures gather sticks
spiky indigo bundles bent at the waist
draped in charcoal and jasmine
south of my keening heart

and three camels go loping
untethered, unburdened, unhurried, carefree
south of my heart where the shale advances
in layers of sandstone and darkening scree
a door in a field fencelessly glinting
south of my solitary heart

the lumbering stork
rising in spirals from her minaret nest
south of my heart at the base of Black Mountain
a one-legged woman draped in blue is
building a bridge across a sandstorm
building a prayer-palm cut short on crutches

set inside an umber wall
lone and roofless beneath
a mud-red river in full flood

                    south of my heart, a gate
        wooded and webbed in simple thatch
            a diamond painted turquoise door

and my father says no, it doesn't hurt him
                he can't even feel his feet
                 and the mica glows deep
              inside the honeycombed sandstone
                replete with swallows and
        the absence of shrines—*O Bequeath*

                from foot to ankle to knee
    the tight balloon thrust of his upper arches
            loosening into foot-sized gloves
              and yes, it's tingling and yes
                it's a nice sort of tingling
                   as he nods his surprise

                    Ay, south of my heart
              where the black shale shingles
      and the red rocks slope in the deepening scree
                         on the high road
                         on the low road
                   on the road through the valley

where my father says yes to the rose oil
which flowers and fades from purple
to yellow his straw-dry skin

to me your Skyclad body
your vaulted bonebox—
sunk so low in the leatherette chair
and we talk saying little, saying much of it
softly watching
the fluid travelling up

south of my heart he lets out a sigh
a long-legged, smoke-coloured sigh
where south of my heart the water
wells in his watery eyes
and he says
There's a first time for everything

my father leans back in his chair
with his left foot
with his right foot
with his earthbound sigh
round as a pigeon headbutting the sheepfold
deep in the palms of my hands

Keep doing whatever you're doing
he says, *we've got time*
we've got plenty of time…

GOLD

Forty Desert Days and Nights in White
All right margin lines in italics are quotes from Anne Carson's *Plainwater* (1995)

Ouyen Caravan Park

Beautiful the nerves pouring around in her like palace fire.

No moon night.
Being held under.
A dark swallow.
The fold of the pillow a shark's.
Face I accept I.

Might not be nearly enough or even.
The deadly living the lively dead.
Beer bottle dance in the next campsite.
Humping the ground so hard so cold with the one artificial.
Electric flower.
Burning all night through.
This tent wall thin as gunpowder.
Stumbling to the toilet block.

Blue neon pole in socks and crocs crackle.
Concrete frost last ever caravan park.
Too many boozed-up grunters I'd rather face whatever ghosts.
Out alone under stars in the sparkling.
Dark moon of my want, or not.

On the B12, after Underbool

How is a pilgrim like an epigram? Ask me tomorrow.

[Hark?] the optimism of a jetty parked in a paddock of dust.
Squinting a red roar through a town with no bread.
But pink lakes and salted algae, breathing.
Purple ranges welcome after a parallax of train tracks and pipelines.
At the no-name petrol stop, I stop two women in saris and gold jewellery who point me to.
Their lean-to bathroom lush with painted grass and plastic string.
The rust-encircled promise of poppy-headed taps.
Air, petrol, ice-cream, tackle, flags and hats.

On the Stuart Highway

*Pilgrims were people who took a surprisingly long time
to cross the head of a pin.*

I looked to the desert and longed to be [Ha!] the wind.
Inside the tumbleweed, tumbling.
All the unknown reasons, the butter in foiled squares.
The maudlin motel ghosts with their shirred shudderings setting off the grey curtains.
Cross-country, the cry inside me not-I [Ha! again].
A keen-tailed kestrel chasing the apostle bird.
Pine trees in flashes of sky-corridors, left and right of the highway darkness.
A coiled snake seen too late sprung between my eyes.

At the Breakaways outside Coober Pedy

The picture has been taken looking directly into the light,
a fundamental error.

How can I not-I.
Paint the changing light in a desert sky at sunset.
Better not try.
Better just sit and let.
Every particle shimmer the jet colourless.
Dogbeams winding up the wildflowers.
Yellow and white, yellow and gold, green turning gold, turning.
Red, no colours in the tin remotely.
The surge (close up) that can't keep up, that surges surging.
Rain falling sideways, a bird's good luck passage, the beams.
Under my boots whole orchestral suites of sky waving deaf arms at.
Solitary figure on Breakaway Mountain shouting from the top of her lungs whatever.
The singing immensity without me in it even more wildly.
Singing.

Campsite, Finke River

"Must get a hat," she would say every time, bending her head. Half smile.

Time a whistling nest of habit and restlessness.
I keep seeing three dimensional triangles inside triangles, the stars.
Vast distances apart and some sort of boat.
Dragging an anchor, this bedroll makes a good seat also!

The cosmic mathematics of not sleeping bursting all around me in tetrahedrons and.
A scattering of foiled potatoes the dingo stole while I must have been sleeping.
Wide and winking nothing has prepared me for this falling.
A night heron slaps the water and swallows a silver fish.

*

At Serpentine Gorge

Water abandons itself.

The smile that rises.
Dark and clear and cold like a rock pool with its own eternal.
Springing where if you swim you might get caught.
In the crosswise spiral.
Waterdrop unwary swimmers go down.

*

At Trephina Gorge

Your separateness could kill you unless I take it from you as a sickness.
What if you get stranded in the town where pears and winter
are variants for one another?

So I send you this orange rock wall.
Flaming as the sun sets in two.
Beats of my heart grown furred and famished.
For you ripe as the moon whose veins.

Swing back under the water bucket.
Handle which snapped and caught the nail.
Sloshing against my chest with a tearing ping.
But though ragged and split away from the skin.

How these hands sing balanced on a rock.
Upside down river beneath.
Bushapple green scented mint.
Crumbled in my pocket and gone in an instant.

The way I would follow you to the ends.
On a flying carpet but don't.
With all this earth thrumming.
Flying ants, humming feet.

Walking from Trephina Gorge

                                                    Some pilgrims drown, some do not. Claro.

Dark blood threading the wild strawberry.
Distance on the tongue the texture of hair and seeds and water.
Tiny scarlet balls startling the green undergrowth, the silent dew.
Drops thirstily on the uphill walk I am getting lost upon.
Days empty my hands empty the prolonged energy of square roots.
The road through the desert is also a causeway is also the ocean charged with.
Withness or is it, I want to know what kind.

To the John Haye's Waterhole

Pilgrims were people who carried little.
They carried it balanced on their heart.

Food trees I don't know the names of.
Though the birds are busy with seed and pod and I recognise some.
Evaporating on the tongue in quick syllables, once-given-gifts, the leavings.
Hovering right and left a level clearing covered in walkers' cairns and.
A red rock shaped like a heart balanced on top of.
Twin triangles pointing in both directions.
[Ha!] so strong the desire to pocket that heart.
I leave the rock where it is pure heat climbing.

And back again

An entrance should be a door built as a kiss.

The almost-full moon swinging close to.
The sun sending royal convoys but still no-show.
In the silver blue (Venus blinking) I climb to.
The beginnings of the ridge-top walk and startling along it six hours one way.
I leave the scree and rocks and spinifex giving way to.

Still walking

You reach out your hand for bread and grasp a stone.

These fine threads that stick love and its dark holdings.
Clear to my face I cut.
The heads off all three snakes with a sharp shovel blade, heart racing.
The last almost invisible squirts blue o why did I kill it?
Thick as a baby's finger I didn't think to fall is to stop wanting.

Pelican Sandbar at Finke River, bush campsite

When is a pilgrim like a photograph?
When the blend of acids and sentiment is just right.

This solitary mango (the sun), the indigo weather, what if.
But my darling the crazy thing is.
Right here impossible true burning all the way through.
My crazy thing.
We are [O].
Touching fingertips whose hearts mutually [Yes/No].
We are forty ribbons whose only common language is.

no wind, yet the windbells
keep on ringing

Taking and failing and making whatever face this strangeness turns.
On us from moon to moon we are.
Given [O] regard the sun as.
[Yes/No] so glorious it hurts and we are here, although.
I am sitting by a river in a desert five times eight thousand away from.

Pilgrims were people glad to take off their clothing,
which was on fire.

The speed of dawn to dusk.
Set so opposite we dance like shadows in the face of our cannot.
[Yes/No] but who can know.
Why the pelicans at Finke float, and circle, and stay.
Darkness threads the ground nightly.
      Not-I [O] this shifting bloom of sand.
We are the astonishment of pelicans so far distant.
Broken open   such close distance   [O] so far inland.

COPPER

Implosion

        smells like a radio.
Fever glands flower
escape hatches
        the forever shores
rip
        & roar.
Isolate
combed crystal,
        a solar
fragrance, the limpid
lake answers the
        tubular [blank].
        Reason
flattens   the hole
        Eclipse.
Nothing much
going on   killing you
by inches.   Hexagonal swards.
        The only wax
between this & this
what the bee makes inside
an ear that has ceased
        straining nausea:
        you won't
hold eye contact but assign
yourself a flower
        alive and mute
like the needle
of a wise and unconscious compass
intent as a puffer fish
ploughing the sand with a single fin

forever against the tide
      a perfect   [   ].
         Or if
    now I am grounded
& doing the splits you pull
on the stumps of what were once
      how many grass blades
can we just   certain things you say
over & over   to keep
      that helicopter
cacophonic fixture   hanging by a
        [   ].

Ode to Sludge

After *the darkness of the now*, a grey
sludge arrives with its barrow load
of wet cement and no amount of lemon zest
will lift it. You'd think dogs and sunshine
just the antidote required to fight
this bone marrow ache that sits like an unwanted
relative at the end of the bed demanding
tea, vodka, cake. Too late.
This one's a real carcass.
No walk in the park in the noontide sun,

this one's a Wolf who's taken up residence
in grandma's slippers and grandpa's face.
No barking's good enough, no soup, no
sun, no new idea, no *top-notch* or *tickety-boo*,
my visitor has, as you'd guess, no manners
and talks non-stop like a bad British sit-com,
mouthing discontent with a furry tongue
that takes pedantic pleasure in every lapsed
Catholic or piece of ugly china. *Smash it!*
this unwelcome guest proclaims, then sinks

like a moth with vampire teeth into any
last camphor-ridden article of faith:
It's all a waste, a pointless sham, tastes like Spam,
the world's unwieldy, boring, late.
No fun taking this one out on any kind of date.
Patience, says my wobbly head, *he'll get*
sick of the grumps when you go to bed,
only he doesn't. This is one Black Dog
who thinks he's found a furever home,
only he never flaps his doggy ears or drools

or throws himself in mud. This one's
no dog, this one's a drug. I grow wily,
a slut for beauty with my face pushed tight
into every flower, Grandpa Drudge
clicking hard at my heels up every hill,
the laps at the pool turned barmy.
He really knows how to cart that barrow.
I need a cloak, not this rasping cough.
I need to hook up a different tomorrow.
The self-help book says naming the monster

helps manage the day: I discover
he's afraid of pokers. I name him Dorian Gray.
Bad move. He just gets younger, more
vigorously vicious. *Go away!* No-can-do,
says Dorian. He's sitting up reading
Grandpa's letters and has taken to wearing
trousers with chequers, polished spats,
silk ties and tweedy caps. Picking peanuts
from his teeth, he tells me I'm looking low
and no, he hasn't anywhere else to go.

Keep going

I took the lift. It went up. I'd forgotten which floor I was meant to be on, even though I'd just asked Linda, *One or four?* So first I went up. Nobody there. Then I went down. Stood in the hallway, pondering. What does Number One? I mean, what is its character? Then I went inside the lift again. Up to where I thought I was going. Sat in a chair. Feet on the floor. Owls on my shirt, *too-whit-to-woo*. In the dark of mourning. Then Lou arrived. With tigers on her skirt. Round and round the banyan tree. Like butter. Shoes, feet, floor, head, a certain number of bags. Also under my eyes. A thousand bowls of butter turned to ghee. That's it. With Suzanne and Linda and Lou and me.

Trespassers Beware of Snakes

I want to be myself, and nobody.
Found in the heart
of the commonest daisy, and in the ditch
where the dead wombat rots,
legs drawn up, pouch open.

I am not saying
I want to die, but to die to the want itself,
that which hustles and hurries us through
the known and the hidden, all this
disastrous desiring—

In tears today, walking the Reservoir wall,
whose waters slash grizzlegrey behind
a barbed wire fence sporting a sign
that lists the numerous venomous
snakes living under the

private-property-keep-out rocks
sloping down to slate,
the wind in its free passage makes
a coloratura between chain-link and sign,
a sound so close to laughter I teeter

precariously on the edge of—
who am I to call upon the moon as I do,
befuddled with loss, and this hole in my belly
that grows and flows even into the guttering
backwash of all the unshed tears that pour—

dry-eyed, your dear face
floats across the water, its melon
of brain wired so differently into
the difference between us, a distance
now given a name, now known by us to be

unchangingly innate. Even as the moss
streaks its burnt fringe down the dry side
of this dam wall, I can accept myself
as neither and nobody, which is how
I enter this emptiness and love you.

Ode to the Not-I

The eye in the pebble spills its secret. (Ask Fellini.)
Every pebble has its purpose, even the stars.
I am the knot in the Not-I in motion.
I am a little eye breaking.

The ginger cat sleeps with one eye open
on the second folded bed under the peeling wallpaper.
How he got here between the locked door
and the sun going down on wherever he goes

in the daytime—I like to think my purpose is
to walk through walls like Peanut, yet I wake
heavy with headache and not even the fake
fur-ball / high-low / what-a-night—Peanut yawns.

Such knots are hard to loosen.
Some keep count, but that was a long time ago.
Others carry stones in their pockets, Not-I.
Mine is an ovoid andesite found on a black-sand

beach that seeps fresh water from a song-licked
cliff-face. The Not-I knows this place from the way
her feet light up like two souls walking
the underside of shadow. What do feet remember?

Only the letting go when Joy shoots up like a geyser
knocking her sideways on hands and knees,
a pitted, perfect stone. Not-I, the hand
that cradles the sun packed with purpose

wearing the sweetest of holes in my pocket.
Ah yes. All the odds uneven.
The knot in the I in motion.
Beautifully jagged, purposefully broken.

Break, / 'the silent life-giver of worlds'[1]
after Frida Kahlo, Jeanette Winterson, and Ralph Waldo Emerson

'Each has a tone like cut glass.'
—Anne Carson

I

    Fine sand calibrates the sound of cut-glass shrinks. What is tone? What is each? The St. Andrew's spider corners a ricrac thread turned delicate. High to the waist in the place where the horses bolted. Once a cut snake teeming with paper boats and kids in tyres, all those slicked and muddy feet. Still a few shards left over. Grass that cuts like paper in spindles pinned with ticks: glassy grass in ricracs, almost a kind of loving. The devil you know. In a screw top jar. Little bit not far. Clean as sand. Plain as mud. Sweet.

II

    Panes of glass. Grass blowing. On the banks of the Todd in flood everything a psychedelic green with hints of acid. But I've got this wrong. The glass is smooth even though it moves slowly down the window one hundred years of loving past the present rate. Windows washed with water. Those microfiber-wonder-cloths that make the glass look clean when wet for half an hour, dry in streaks like finger painting: glass grown thin and thickened at the base, framed by boards soft-grained and holding tightly to bending straight. But I've got this wrong.
    Think: water music. Think: fountains. Think: how do they keep the glass clean on all those pretty cake counters. I never felt cleaner covered in sand those forty days in a car beside her. Salt crusts the skin and catches the glass on fire. We brushed the flakes off and walked on water without the cake picking up the taste of disinfectant or rubber gloves or the paper they use to serve the pretty cakes on. I've got this wrong. I've got to keep things plain as mud.

III

Sappho, why is the moon rising in the upper corner of the triangle window at half-past ten in the morning? I would have thought *I had a name, but I have forgotten it.*² Have I fed the cat? Has *anyone* fed the cat? The cat says *N-e-oow,* convincingly.

The icy sluice lifts bare feet through mist whose shortest of days glows briefly. Soft midday winter half-past noon and she writes to say she loves the impossible as Goethe does, that yearning for the impossible is quite possibly what she loves most in me quite. What for others might. Patience: how can I muster it. I might make a bust of it.

In clay.

Batteries, keys, glasses, cake. Think: Kahlo. Think: Kit Kat.

*Morning breaks, the friendly reds, the big blues, hands full of leaves, fingers in the hair, pigeons.*³ She is impossible. The cat had a name once, but I think she's forgotten it. The second cat's name is. She's a wild one, Sappho. *A main lesson of wisdom to know your own from another's.*⁴ I think that's her second breakfast. I trust you to make. *Gladly we would anchor but the anchorage is quicksand.*⁵ Water runs fiercely beneath. Breaking only to break. Out of glass. Which rivers dryly down the centuries and thickens. *The universe is the bride of the soul.*⁶ Like chocolate. All the pretty cakes and all the pretty horses turning south. The icy river sluices bare feet plain and sweet. *My hands are sunk in oranges*⁷ which the cloud-cobbled wind blows fresh off the mountain in a eucalypt blizzard. If wishes were horses *the particoloured wheel must revolve very fast to appear white.*⁸

She writes to say the poets I am reading found god in female form the most perfect. Terrified of the ecstasy of whirling. She writes to say keep whirling. Your impossible is perfect. The cosmic telegraph is working. Snow flurries the orange blossoms my hands are sunk. Yes, the windcaps are wine cups, could almost be—what do you think a soul is made of? Cracks in the concrete a wild mustard. Waterhole up the mountain nobody goes to. Long-time-little-bit not-far they put a fence around it. The deer always find a way through, though. And the ducks keep whirring their emeralds. Stray feathers float the broken pylons. Somebody is singing the country up there. Somebody must be singing it. The water, I tell you, the water is surely alive.

1	Frida Kahlo	4	Ralph Waldo Emerson	7	Frida Kahlo
2	Jeanette Winterson	5	Ibid	8	Ralph Waldo Emerson
3	Frida Kahlo	6	Ibid		

Ode to Earth

In her speaking she returns to us and I,
with my Not-I awake, and going about my day,
walk with Earth behind my lids, two by two,
and breathing thus, she holds us by the feet.
                      Today, between the work of marking
                      someone else's words and the turning
                      of vegetables to bread, Earth took me out
                      and placed me in one resistless sweep
deep beneath her shining, whose lips on mine
she parts the shine and spins the Not-I surface
calm and sleek. There she holds and there
she takes a parting of the ways I cannot
                      name it. Though I crave it, the ten thousand
                      ways she tastes, unspooling Byzantium between
                      my ribs, her soft camel lashes brush the knap
                      of the Not-I that soars unmade in me
and wings me back to hearth beneath
a younger Earth snapped open: a whale's
pelvis rocking the deep beneath the desert
un-sea-ed in me, the not-mine
                      taking me thoroughly in pieces with it:
                      charcoal, date-seed, ash and silicon,
                      the dunes with their kelp and nautilus,
                      potassium, all the spinning glow worms
unseen for centuries, curled in torchlight, whose
good wood burns great sliding prints on damp
cave walls chanting the riverborn heartsnake
welling upwards: the ten by ten

                    by thousand-year ice in rock and sand,
                    the windstorm in my rib-bones untangling
                    the tendrils of this beetroot's roots, the slim
                    carrots and the parsley rinsed under a rustling
tap, whose pouring on my fingers is rain! rain
stored and steeped in sweetness, that unmistakeable
skyspeech swinging through the water barrel: hello
Earth again, here we are getting on with dinner
                          ten thousand light years later in less than half a day.
                          Smoke rises through the roof you grew in patience,
                          holding your softness out, wanting us
                          to love you, wanting us to love
your night touch turning your breath diaphanous,
oh yes, the way the not-I draws upright to meet you
as water draws such thirst from stars they pour
your breathing hands upon our feet.

Notes on a Sunday night before sleeping

A gecko slips under the fold
where cushion meets cushion on an old
corded sofa perfect for reading
and as I read, I half-expect a flurry
                                    of fine lizard feet on ankles, bookish
                                    hands or neck, yet what happens next
                                    is even finer: that portal latched to darkness
                                    swings on webs, which humming-
birds collect inside my chest
where starlings build their crystal nests
out of their own saliva. Here I rest,
spanned by bats, and ropes of notes
                                    that plant the singing egg in each to
                                    each: a thousand airborne nests
                                    the size of human baby-hearts
                                    in utero rapidly pumping. But then,
and here's the hook, I read how
these caves, once discovered, soon
descend into the sending of children up
for bird-egg soup collected in a sack
                                    sold on the black market for some
                                    outrageous sum by the tonne,
                                    enough to build cathedrals
                                    in the mouth of darkness, and yet
prairie owls coat their doorsteps
with simple dung, and dung beetles
become a walking larder, rolling
their own cocoa-coated eggs away

                    and I think of the bamboo rat who
                    harvests the freshening shoot by pulling on
                    a ceiling root and hauling underground
                    the ripening stalk for later. How a poem
should be no less a bean
the handy size of a small grenade
gnawed by teeth packed with stardust
and the stealth of dung stowed in
                    careful cosmic caves inside the heart
                    grown mutinous, resistance swarming
                    into life with the pin pulled out
                    already bursting into flower.

SILVER

Alphabet Unskinned: a Reader
after Jenny Watson, Georgia O'Keefe, Fiona Woods, Thich Quang Duc and Haruki Murakami

Azoth or apocatastasis?
cat's eye   pyramid   mountain tunnel
mineshaft to   dew bug
            dancing star

Boiled eggs still burning
in a pot forgotten on a stove
out walking
the blackened pages
scored in skin
my heart in danger (tender-tangled)
still requires Goya's
naming of the thing—
as a hound pup
learns to read the burning
on the wind, so too the shock
of first inhaling that peculiar scent,
protein packed / not to be
confused with innocence …

>**Cells remember.**
>
>As do kitchens and firepits,
>the grease
>built up through past-life fires
>on coated rims, the way
>neurons blaze at
>highchair angled, heeldrummed

　　　　　　　　　　　　　yellow, the simple
　　　　　　　　　　　　　taste of buttered corn on a silkwarm
　　　　　　　　　　　　　cob, pricked and furry, mistaken
　　　　　　　　　　　　　rightly at aged three for love.

Does death require
desire skinning through
the open-eye effect?
　　　　　　To differentiate
angelic shades of lack, I cast my own
and try to call the answer back
accepting failure
~~I should have known~~
I was always going Home
　　　in answer
　　　　　to bewildered Job
(devoted / diligent / damage-packed)
call it what you will

Eclipsed
　　　　　~~erasure~~
　　　　　　　[the I/not-I nevertheless
　　　　　defiant　　　　　　　undoing [Gladys / my goodness /
　　　{un}expectantly

Fiona Woods, on the other hand, demands
that the work should be　　　to strive to answer what we still
don't know　　to serve　　those who come tomorrow
　　　　[the ghost of Georgia O'Keeffe on repeat:
　　　　Whether you succeed or not, there is no such thing. Making

     your unknown known is the important thing—and keeping the unknown always
      beyond you.
What gives our bodies shape? Professor Woods suggests it's
     skin. Also,
     There is no point in getting up in the morning to be average,
as she phenomenally demonstrates.
     This is the true joy in life she says, quoting Shaw, *the being*
     used for a purpose recognised by yourself as a mighty one. The being
     a force of nature instead of a feverish little clod
     of ailments and grievances, complaining that the world
     will not devote itself to making you happy.   Ah Fiona,
[George meet Georgia,   I thank thee.   Affectionately,
     Striving
     for excellence is the responsibility of everyone.
Meanwhile, Anh Do
(fronting the new face of the ABC)   paints her with his palette knives
while they discuss   the three-dimensionality of skin.

Goodness
is as goodness knows
     ~~I know it~~
     Good for the greater good of the smallest one
     among us but what is
goodness?   Astute to the necessary shadow
   (in service to whom? [I/not-I
     ~~grow Grace~~   from time to time   but for whom
the Gladys?
   stumbling full face into cowpats
     good god   and all the goddesses

Hold fire.

I,

    Jenny Watson, *Rockstar*
    having served successfully this fickle world of art going on
    more than forty-five years now and I'll have you know *it's not all skittles and beer.*
    The end result is a painting, but you can still sense the movement that went into it.
    Finished painting is not something I'm particularly interested in.
    I want the footprint of *how it was made to remain obvious.*

Knowing the steps
    I go my own way. I did / did not
        wake up in a gutter with blood on my face. I did sleep a lot. I did cry
  Ladders, after all   go both ways, and

      Matter matters just as much in Sky City,   if not more.

      Nemesis, however, is always already material.

Only a man could order
another man to skin a living man
while keeping that living man
alive for a time / for a time.

          Evil makes a sound in the throat
          that masquerades as mercy: first
          one tender sleeve removed
          ~~and then~~ [no sequence orders sense

the scream that ruptures ~~no name~~
~~to~~ pain   the other like a glove
       goes on screaming into un-
Consciousness regained

                 and [I/Not-I
                 push the book away from torso skin
                 [~~my~~ nipples still intact   laid out
                 beside the man without a word

a seam   his lips and nose
and testicles removed   no name
uttered ~~what is the~~   [no]Thing
gained /   [~~the hinge~~

                 ~~in every chronicle?~~   until even the one
                 who ordered the skinning begins to
                 suspect the One   being
                 skinned never knew

(not true)   and the man on his knees
who could be next   who is [Not-I
vomiting until there is nothing left
[is] spared or almost *at least not skinned*

                 but who can say what becomes of him
                 forced to watch (or I?)   still retching
                 and what   becomes of   ~~to become~~
                 the tender hidden manifold [~~negated~~] one

who pours   the seams left open
~~the mind still reading/reeling~~ when faced
with the choice of a leap into darkness
or a bullet on the count of five?

                       Does it help   [~~no it doesn't~~]   not
                       knowing if the missing man survived?
                       [I keep on seeing   a three-or-thirty-second Sun
                       [what have Murakami's wells begun?

Please,
I'm just a suburban Girl pushing my father in a wheelchair

       'hell bent on escape from quite a young age'

[But give me air   I woke up and *'Being human and particularly being a girl*
human, growing up in the suburbs   *I decided to put in the whole shebang, the whole*
mess'—I

QUESTION   the definite article   for instance the

Rainbow in the mirror   of a horse's flank   [to whom does the rain bow?
and when I went to

Spider Rock
    Etcetera [vertigo in the belly: [O] how now / brown owl
                            and then/and then/and then

The fiction that slaughters
the blindness in me is also the blindness
I taste and see in boiled eggs and smoke and stones a smell   I carry in the sweat of my own *miedo*   [*fear* of *what?*   here already   walking   marrowed through my ~~whale~~ bones
this bulky baulking out walking
and not talking about the dizziness that falls
and falling through the daily things
burnt hair burning that bad egg smell
though some have skin and some have not and this is the hell I cannot repay this
is the debt I cannot delay this falling
falling through the blackened house a terror so nameless so peeling true only the falling ~~(not even the falling)~~ nothing but falling can carry us   through [but to which ~~intransitive verb~~ if ~~not~~ here am I going?

Undertow   or is it / am i
         less Rananim and more
               Cyclone Fence with Great Dane (1972)?

      You don't say.   [But what about the colour blue.
           Says who?

VERTIGO
                                  this intractable Is-ness is all I'm left with

When scalded, place the wound
under cool flowing water for at least
twenty minutes   [years   nebulae
                  Do not apply ice.

                X marks the spot.
                    [~~to burn~~

Y does it?   In *Painting for a Man Who Likes His Privacy* (1993) a female figure stands with her back turned, her red hair a flaming rectangle, not for him,

Zenobia, those pearls that were your—
            'it's an illusion that lasts for a particle of time.'

The Pretty Face of Domesticity (2014)   crawling in a yellow dress

      through the caged and vertical wallpaper
      [here comes the definite indefinite

           Touch My Skeleton (2014)
           Eye of the Storm (1984)

MERCURY

Cusp

Oak tree
I want to be
after ash
born bare

branches that catch
gold on the road
in the cold afternoon
more dazzling

than the raw leek bulbs
turning the bones
of the disembowelled
owl swept under

steps like a leaf sprung
to shade the back-
porch tap, the squat
dry wash rustling

a flicker of cat,
clear and cold and clean.
I want your leaf breath.
I want to lean.

Wings
after Wim Wenders' *Wings of Desire*

for Bonny Cassidy

When does the beat of the first heart start?
When does flow overflow and not get stuck and go on flowing?
How do angels choose their names?
Will I ever ken the wind of when?
In time, I am a child, not yet begun, counting the meadows.
Once upon, when time without end, and then and then and then.
In duplicate, on stools, in stems.
Twirling like decadent umbrellas.
The we before the why in the when.
To pivot inside the sun's great eye and turning, behold, become.
Creamy tactility in monochrome and rich cream buns.
Damiel, Cassiel, Haniel, Uriel.
Gabriel, Michael, Raphael, Zadkiel.
Strange the sterility of insomniac libraries,
the delicate, listening pen.
To fall through time textured as a silk stocking.
The armour that split the infinitive falling.
The armour, all hollowed, that fell.
Amour made Thou: ruby red, the touch
of blood from your armour-struck head
a choice, the salt
on your tongue-licked hand.
Empty sandpit tracked wide in grayday drag.
Trenchcoat, no suitcase, tramping.
Hot coffee steaming, the rub
of not thinking the beat of the infinite why.
Bluered grown bold, a love of the cold
walking into full colour: learning to read

painted letters on a wall, the twelfth no longer
the same (*don't jump, dear soul,* hand on a shoulder,
the man still jumped) no longer the end of your name.
What do we choose? What is my task please help me remember, I
am already forgetting again.

Bread

after the textile artist Melinda Heale's exhibition, *Dyeing the Liminal*

for Kathryn Nevell

Take a cup of nodding bristlegrass
between two stones and grind
the flat into the heart
of the round which has weathered

its way out of the ground.
Take then the dewy flame
of whichever nasturtium comes to hand
for its practical peppery taste

and the tears it draws from the air
each morning. Mix a little of these
with your own. The paste
will thicken as all good dough does

if you let it alone in its rising.
And this manna shall be blessed
by all manner of thing, as a blue
lotus is blessed by that which opens

a guarded throat.
Unguard your throat.
Let the blue brim.
When set in sunlight

and baked in the shape
of your very own hunger
break a little
and return to the ground

the heart of the bowl
you grind from.
As recipes go, the flavour
of gratitude is nutty and sweet,

and the anise of thanks shall fleck
this pocket bread with frankincense.
Eat every last crumb
with a lightened heart, or give

at least half to your neighbour.
This is a seed bread, a weed bread,
hand-garnered from ground
and the light that leavened it.

Don't hoard it.
But if you need to travel a long way
on a lonesome and dusty road,
take this bread in your pocket

and sing with it.
It will never go off.
It will never go mouldy. This bread
freshens even the beauty of silk.

Sappho

She is sweeping the bricks.
She is tending the sea.
She is mending the mud of her
mind-meadowed asylum.
She is forty-one hundred and three.

Breathe little Scarab,
shake your antlers and fart
like a fish. This too shall—
all manner of thing—my feral
cumquat, my Saha, my flirt.

She swabs with her broom
all manner of plastic, brings it
to harbour, turns it to light.
Feels her mouth water, hauling
it in, the flight

of the pelican astride the wind.
She is sweeping the bricks.
She is calling the cat.
She is eating a sandwich
in her sun-fingered flat.

Finding a banknote.
Paying a bill.
Humming a half-note,
standing still.
Out beyond the breakers,

where ideas of wrong
doing and right turn into
there is a field
of plastic the size of France
swaying like heavenly plankton.

Her soul lies down in that grass,
cradling the kitten who leapt
from a first-floor balcony,
just like that, when the world
was too full to talk about.

She is touching the rapids
of that starry heart beating.
She is finding the finitude
of blood in a sneeze.
She is vetting the path.

She is bowing to mud.
She is counting the neon
in gulls' feet and gloves.
The arthritic acrylics
of her grandmother's rug.

The gutters are gushing,
the kitten intact. She is losing
the albatross, and hauling it in.
She is casting her heart
on oar-strokes of wind.

Lacuna

Over Christmas, he caught her
in the act
of disappearing, reached out,
planted a kiss on her mouth,
and said, *Go*.
Into snatched nowhere-ness
she wandered,
landing eventually on hot grass
under a ticking banksia.
The ants soon made tunnels
in the dirt where she lay.
The dam, in its shrinking, gurgled mud.
She saw in her mind the long succession
of kitchens and cars she'd done time in.
Someone sent a child out to call her in.
I'm hungry, the child said.
What I would like, the sister-in-law said.
Why don't you, the man who was trying to
unlearn how to be her husband said.
All day, and through the many days,
she moved through pockets
of scorching shade and the cool unceasing
demands within. *No*,
she said, *I am resting*, she said, *someone
else's turn*, she said. The house
shook with their voices raised
in three languages, everyone talking
and no one listening to the smallest
among them saying, *I am hungry, please
Auntie*. Little by little, she answered
each need with the ferocity of termites

collapsing the kitchens inside her,
counting the days while tending
the children, the children, other
people's children, while they smoked
and lolled in her hammock
and complained about the food.
Between one decade and the next,
having spent five minutes in midday sun
screaming silently in a paddock of butterflies,
this woman, no longer corralled
by mother or wife or girl, clearly heard
a high-pitched clicking sound
coming up out of the ground.

Tidal

It's the hour of the day when you stop trying.
When the sea turns its back to the wall.
When waves utter roundness, but slowly.
When the torpor of old city silks.
The hour when traffic implodes moving backwards.
When dogs go strolling with people on leads.
When the indigo light climbs through holes like a crab's fist.
When ships drain the harbour, when plazas of sand.
A skater with ear buds etches hashtags on concrete.
Bins full of plastic rub shoulders with glass.
It's the hour of almost, of tunnels, of turtles,
of matter that later you almost outlast.

One

after *One Infinity*, Beijing Dance Theatre's and Dance North Australia's premiere dance performance, Malthouse Theatre, October 2018

for Loveday Rose Why

To write with a horsehair brush
dipped in water on bare boards, air
dissolves in a moment the poem
that has entered, and altered,
the quantum field.

A dancer, too, slips into
and through that invisible
eddy, swirls and triangles
beneath a floodlit slow crawl
upward through millennia: the stew

inside the cocoon a choreography
of light: cloud-fish, wildebeest,
nautilus flood, wild murmuration,
flesh, bone, muscle, blood. I
was charged by wild horses once,

tearing through a field of burning
grass, heads held high and tails
streaming their glance
on me as they thundered past
both a promise and a warning:

the sheer ecstasy of the ground
shaking their starry hooves.

Breath

As when walking yesterday's
catastrophic dawn, the surf
a cauldron turned wild and brown,
two pelicans rowed the air like floating
parentheses and swept with purpose
the high, sweet, cold-fronted wind.
I want nothing less than to be
blessed by poems such as these
that breathe with the soul's hands
and feet. As when I lay my hands
on a woman's back and she lets
out a breath like a dreaming forest
and I feel the sky step
toward her as she lets, without labour,
her breath back in. As when her
trapezius flutters like a manta ray
coming to stillness in the dozing depths,
and I feel the breath she lets roll through her,
the full winged scapular
softenings that open her rhomboids
like flowers. As when the deer
decides it is safe to step
into her very own
moonfresh meadow
through the velvet, permissible dark,
there on the underbreath I follow
without sight, by touch alone, the deep
heart's mysterious rose, the rare
treasures it lifts from the very back
of the heart that hardly gets touched,
or not enough, oh, there, at last, at long

last, the deer remembers
how to drink the tenderest dew
in that moonwashed and radiant field.

Questions

At birth, the bird flew high and white
and motionless, the eye of the storm not yet
arrived but drawing nearer, the bird
loose in its orb of stillness branching
its wings in the hospital hallway between
the lights going out and the generator
roughly clanking the lights back on, in that
moment of cyclonic noise subsiding, the veil
your mother reached down to touch
between the legs they had raised in stirrups
above her, slid warm, unbroken, and when
she, frightened, drew you to her, only a
makeshift curtain pulled partially
around the trolley where they had
parked her, alone and shaved, one among
many, young, untaught, she felt
before she saw, like glistening gladwrap,
the bag you came in, and she held you in it,
horrified, believing in that moment before
the light flooded you with ultraviolet,
that you were gone from her, or dead, or worse,
a creature from another universe, which was
partly true and partly all she could feel through
in that overrun, clamorous place, but then you
reached your curled fist palm-upwards,
and kicked to break that sticky breach of trust
and rushed her skin, which bloomed
beneath you, and in that transom, your tiny
ovaries quickened like stardust
and she saw in your unblinking eyes
not the surprise of the unseen bird

like a torn sail above her, but something
pass wing-shadowed through your widened
pupils, and she pitied the mewl you made
and brought herself to love you.

Notes

These poems were composed cyclically over a five-year period spent learning and thinking about alchemy, dark matter and heart country. The question I set myself when I began this book may well have been: 'In light of this task set before me, which I take as the task to love, how am I to live?' This is not a new question. No poem in this collection was written before it was walked: arbitrary or otherwise, the rule I applied to this book's organic growth was that each poem was to be 'discovered' on foot, and many continued to be composed peripatetically across many drafts while out walking in ways dedicated to that terrain. Composed on unceded lands, I wish to acknowledge and honour the original custodians, Elders and ancestors in places as diverse as New Mexico, Morocco, Millgrove, The MacDonnell Ranges (East and West), New Zealand, Newcastle (NSW), and Jerez (Spain). The following notes attempt to track quoted sources of inspiration, or attributions of work published in earlier forms: any mistakes, or misrememberings, I hereby acknowledge as my own.

※

'Foxstruck': *HMS Sirius* (1786) was the name of flagship of the First Fleet to settle Europeans in New South Wales. 'Sweetened damper' was the euphemism used by early settlers to refer to the practice of putting poison in bread (damper) and distributing to First Nations peoples as an act of genocide in order to steal land. This poem was first published in *Australian Poetry Journal,* 5:2, 2015 and subsequently published in *Best Australian Poems 2016,* Ed. Sarah Holland-Batt, 2016, 112.

'Absent Self Portrait': quotes a line, 'Turn towards emptiness', from the poem 'The desert has many teachings' by Mechtild of Madgeburg, (1207 – 1282?), found in *Women in Praise of the Sacred*, Ed. Jane Hirshfield, New York, Harper Collins, c1994. 'Absent Self Portrait' was shortlisted for the Judith Wright Overland Poetry Award in 2017.

'Fritter the Fat then Fry It' was first published in *The Hunter Anthology of Contemporary Australian Feminist Poetry,* Bonny Cassidy and Jessica L. Wilkinson (Eds), Hunter Publishers, St. Lucia: Qld, 2016, 64-7.

'Black Door with Snow': 'Dot' in this poem refers to Dorothy Porter (1954-2008) Australian poet, verse novelist and lyricist, while 'Black Door with Snow' refers to the image of the black door in the eponymous painting by Georgia O'Keeffe. This poem was first published in *Australian Book Review,* June-July 2017, 62.

'Goat's Cheese with Honey and Rosemary on Toast on a Sunday Morning': quotes lines from Gaston Bachelard's *The Psychoanalysis of Fire* (1964).

'The Glimpse' won the 2016 University of Canberra Health Poetry Prize and was first published in *Meniscus,* 4.2, 2016, 3.

'Errancy: a Primer' was first published in *Verge: Errance,* Monash University Press, 2015, 79-82 and takes its cue from *Emily Dickinson: The Complete Poems*, edited by Thomas H. Johnson (1976).

'As We Spiral Pine Tree Mountain' was first published in *Transnational Literature,* 9:2, May 2017.

'In the Rothko Room at the Tate' was first published in *Australian Poetry Journal,* 7:2, 2018, 51

'Forty Desert Days and Nights in White': 'no wind, yet the windbells / keep on ringing' is a line from the poet Shiren, in Carson's *Plainwater* (1995). This poem was awarded Runner-up in the Newcastle Poetry Prize in 2017.

'Implosion': the lines 'alive and mute like the needle of a wise and unconscious compass' come from Clarice Lispector's *A Breath of Life,* translated from the Portuguese by Johnny Lorenz and edited by Benjamin Moser, 2012.

'Break / 'the silent life-giver of worlds': quotes lines from Frida Kahlo, Jeanette Winterson and Ralph Waldo Emerson.

'Notes on a Sunday night before sleeping' was first published in *Plumwood Mountain Journal of Ecopoetry and Ecopoetics,* 5: 2, 2018.

'Alphabet Unskinned: a Reader': source notes from [Erased] Photo-Images in alphabetical order as follows:

Azoth or Apocatastasis:
Author's photograph of a solo butterfly feasting on a turd in the sunshine taken on the El Calderon Loop Trail, El Malpais National Monument, New Mexico

Does ~~Desire~~?:
Author's photograph of a courtyard inside Sky City, Pueblo of Acoma, New Mexico

Eclipsed ~~erasure~~:
Image of solar eclipse taken from:
http://www.zmescience.com/other/australia-solar-eclipse-14112012/
and linked to Dr. Kate Russo, self-proclaimed 'eclipse-chaser': www.psychologytoday.com/blog/brainstorm/201708/kate-russo-wants-experience-the-solar-eclipse-you

Fiona Melanie Wood:
'Fiona Melanie Wood AM (born 2 February 1958) is a British-born plastic surgeon working in Perth, Western Australia. She is the director of the Royal Perth Hospital burns unit and the Western Australia Burns Service. In addition, Wood is also a clinical professor with the School of Paediatrics and Child Health at the University of Western Australia and director of the McComb Research Foundation.' (Wikipedia) Professor Wood AM was the Australian of the Year in 2005. She is most renowned for her development of "spray-on" skin, a skin cell treatment for burns victims, which enabled her to save many of the Australian Bali bomb victims who came under her care.

Hold Fire:
Internet image of the Immolation of Thich Quang Duc:
http://image.sggp.org.vn/w840/uploaded/dataimages/original/images113984_thichquangduc.jpg

I,:
Image of a detail of a painting, Jenny Watson *Rock Star* (detail) 2014 oil, synthetic polymer paint and Japanese pigment on rabbit skin glue primed damask; vintage plaster duck. Courtesy the artist and Galerie Transit, Mechelen © the artist, https://www.mca.com.au/whatson/2017-7-8/?flavour=primavera

Jenny Watson:
The Fabric of Fantasy, exhib. cat. Museum of Contemporary Art, Australia, MCA, Sydney, 2017.

Knowing:
Author's photograph of salt encrusted granite steps taken while walking the summit of the El Morro National Monument, New Mexico. Quote references a piece of text in Jenny Watson's painting, *The Key Painting* (1987).

Ladders:
Author's photograph of a ladder leading to a rooftop inside Sky City, New Mexico.

Matter:
Author's photograph of a favourite dwelling-place inside Sky City, New Mexico.

Nemesis:
Author's photograph in the carpark of the Sky City Cultural Centre and Haakú Musuem, Pueblo Acoma, New Mexico.

Only:
Text references Haruki Murakami's novel, *The Wind-Up Bird Chronicle*, (1994-1995).
Image is a detail from one of Goya's Caprichos. [Francisco Goya y Lucientes Los Caprichos, Plate 39 *Asta su Abuelo*. 1799. On Loan to the Hamburg Kunsthalle, Hamburg, Germany.]

Please:
'hell bent on escape from quite a young age' (Watson in Dow, 2017). Steve Dow, *Art Guide Australia*, 1 November 2017.

Question:
Author's photograph depicting a face in the cliffs at the base of the El Morro National Monument, New Mexico.

Rainbows:
Author's photograph of a perfectly double rainbow encasing Mt. Little Jo taken at home while writing this erased-photo-poem-essay.

Spider Rock:
Author's photograph of the dizzying vista of Spider Rock in Canyon de Chelly National Monument, north-eastern Arizona. The Diné (Navajo) and Hopi peoples hold their own sacred stories regarding this rock, which narrate the cosmic and demonic deeds of the powerful Spider Woman who resides there.

Under vow:
Author's photograph of the painting by Dorothy Eugenie Brett, *Albedia*, housed in the Harwood Museum of Art, Taos, New Mexico. D.H Lawrence's vision of 'Rananim' is also referenced here. For a comedy of errors regarding (non)utopian relationships, read:
http://www.santafenewmexican.com/pasatiempo/art/from-bloomsbury-to-taos-painter-dorothy-brett/article_4b332a88-7f48-5485-8a2d-21e393003699.html
Jenny Watson's painting, *Cyclone Fence with Great Dane* (1972), oil and acrylic on ten-ounce cotton duck.

Vertigo:
Consists of author's photographs of D.H. Lawrence's iconic Ponderosa Pine tree at 'Rananim', the D. H. Lawrence Ranch in Taos County, New Mexico; a Pinterest image of Georgia O'Keeffe's (iconic, yet realist) 1929 painting, 'The Lawrence Tree', https://es.pinterest.com/pin/321233385902062278/; and author's photograph of homestay breakfast chairs beneath Our Lady of Guadalupe.

Y:
Author's photograph of New Mexican artist's Bob Hauzous' sculpture 'Lady with Pike', situated in front of the Laboratory of Anthropology on Museum Hill, Santa Fe, New Mexico.
Reference to Jenny Watson's *Painting for a Man Who Likes His Privacy* (1993)

Zenobia:
Historically, a third-century queen of the Palmyrene Empire in Syria, juxtaposed in the author's ekphrastic imagination with images of Jenny Watson's *The Pretty Face of Domesticity* (2014), *Touch My Skeleton* (2014 at MCA, Sydney © the artist) and Jenny Watson's *Eye of the Storm* (1984, oil, synthetic polymer paint and coins on canvas, Ross Bonthorne Collection, courtesy and © the artist) and a fragment of her striking quote from the exhibition catalogue, *The Fabric of Fantasy*, Museum of Contemporary Art Australia, p. 156.

'Alphabet Unskinned: a Reader' was first published in the Newcastle Poetry Prize Anthology, 2019.

'Bread' was inspired by the work of Melinda Heal in her exhibition *Dyeing the Liminal*, discovered at *Timeless Textiles: Centre of Fibre Artisans*, Newcastle (2019). In this exhibition, Heal draws on traditional Japanese dyeing techniques to depict Japanese weeds on silk, and departs from tradition in her methods when exploring the painting of Australian weeds on silk using ground-up stones to create pigment from the rocks and soils surrounding the weeds she found in location, while tracing personal sites of significance.

Question:
Author's photograph depicting a face in the cliffs at the base of the El Morro National Monument, New Mexico.

Rainbows:
Author's photograph of a perfectly double rainbow encasing Mt. Little Jo taken at home while writing this erased-photo-poem-essay.

Spider Rock:
Author's photograph of the dizzying vista of Spider Rock in Canyon de Chelly National Monument, north-eastern Arizona. The Diné (Navajo) and Hopi peoples hold their own sacred stories regarding this rock, which narrate the cosmic and demonic deeds of the powerful Spider Woman who resides there.

Under vow:
Author's photograph of the painting by Dorothy Eugenie Brett, *Albedia*, housed in the Harwood Museum of Art, Taos, New Mexico. D.H Lawrence's vision of 'Rananim' is also referenced here. For a comedy of errors regarding (non)utopian relationships, read:
http://www.santafenewmexican.com/pasatiempo/art/from-bloomsbury-to-taos-painter-dorothy-brett/article_4b332a88-7f48-5485-8a2d-21e393003699.html
Jenny Watson's painting, *Cyclone Fence with Great Dane* (1972), oil and acrylic on ten-ounce cotton duck.

Vertigo:
Consists of author's photographs of D.H. Lawrence's iconic Ponderosa Pine tree at 'Rananim', the D. H. Lawrence Ranch in Taos County, New Mexico; a Pinterest image of Georgia O'Keeffe's (iconic, yet realist) 1929 painting, 'The Lawrence Tree', https://es.pinterest.com/pin/321233385902062278/; and author's photograph of homestay breakfast chairs beneath Our Lady of Guadalupe.

Y:
Author's photograph of New Mexican artist's Bob Hauzous' sculpture 'Lady with Pike', situated in front of the Laboratory of Anthropology on Museum Hill, Santa Fe, New Mexico.
Reference to Jenny Watson's *Painting for a Man Who Likes His Privacy* (1993)

Zenobia:
Historically, a third-century queen of the Palmyrene Empire in Syria, juxtaposed in the author's ekphrastic imagination with images of Jenny Watson's *The Pretty Face of Domesticity* (2014), *Touch My Skeleton* (2014 at MCA, Sydney © the artist) and Jenny Watson's *Eye of the Storm* (1984, oil, synthetic polymer paint and coins on canvas, Ross Bonthorne Collection, courtesy and © the artist) and a fragment of her striking quote from the exhibition catalogue, *The Fabric of Fantasy*, Museum of Contemporary Art Australia, p. 156.

'Alphabet Unskinned: a Reader' was first published in the Newcastle Poetry Prize Anthology, 2019.

'Bread' was inspired by the work of Melinda Heal in her exhibition *Dyeing the Liminal*, discovered at *Timeless Textiles: Centre of Fibre Artisans*, Newcastle (2019). In this exhibition, Heal draws on traditional Japanese dyeing techniques to depict Japanese weeds on silk, and departs from tradition in her methods when exploring the painting of Australian weeds on silk using ground-up stones to create pigment from the rocks and soils surrounding the weeds she found in location, while tracing personal sites of significance.

Acknowledgements

Many thanks to the editors of the following journals, anthologies and magazines, and the judges of the following prizes and awards, in which some of these poems have previously appeared, sometimes in earlier permutations.

Australian Book Review
Australian Poetry Journal
Best Australian Poems 2016
Going Down Swinging
Meniscus
New Zealand Poetry Shelf
Plumwood Mountain Journal of Ecopoetry and Ecopoetics
Prayers of a Secular World
Rabbit
Southerly
Soft Serve: Newcastle Poetry Prize Anthology 2019
Transnational Literature
The Crows in Town: Newcastle Poetry Prize Anthology, 2017
The Hunter Anthology of Contemporary Australian Feminist Poetry
Transnational Literature
Underneath: The University of Canberra's International Poetry Prize 2015
Verge 2015: Errance
Westerly
2016 University of Canberra Health Poetry Prize Winner
2016 Judith Wright Overland Prize Shortlisting
2017 Newcastle Poetry Prize Runner-Up
2018 Venie Holmgren Poetry Prize Winner

The title of the artwork on the cover is *New Moon to New Moon, September 37°20'33.4"S 175°30'30.5"E*, a contact print by New Zealand based photographer and artist Kate van der Drift. This work is from a series of camera-less photographs called *Directional Listening: Fluvial Field Notes*. A durational accretion, these images are made by burying large format sheet film in the liminal zone of the Piako river, between the ebb and flow of the low and high tides. Pollution and nutrients from intensive agriculture mix with organic matter and microorganisms, producing clouds of vivid alchemical reactions. The sensitive photographic surface is colonised by Piako's unique mix of elements, algae and bacteria. Kate Van der Drift won the 2020 Uxbridge Estuary Art Award for her innovative ecological work in *Directional Listening: Fluvial Field Notes*. I thank you Kate for your vision and heart in gracing the cover with this gorgeous river print.

Special appreciation goes to those who hosted me at various intervals and who showed all kinds of encouragement and gifted hospitality along the way; some of you were strangers on the road and I never knew your name but I thank you in deeper and deeper appreciation for the gifts that keep on giving across the years. Special gratitude goes to Karen Hadfield and Youssef Bouchedor at Café Tissardmine, whose kindness and consideration knew no bounds (vale Youssef, you will never be forgotten); to Yvette Holt who opened her working home at Hermannsburg Historic Precinct and allowed me to glimpse what could not have been imagined otherwise; to Penny Drysdale, who gave me ballast in Alice Springs; to Constanza Ceruti who said that I could, and kept on saying so; to the many new friends and colleagues met alongside the ghost of Georgia O'Keeffe at Ghost Ranch, New Mexico (I will never forget those cloud horses on the porch each evening, nor the choir who practiced with the birds at sundown), thank you for the sweetness of your company; to David Musgrave and Wendy James who helped me make Newcastle feel like home and who continue to do so; to Nina Massarik, for a magical weekend in your London home and for traipsing around with me through some of your favourite haunts; to Tania Goh, old friend, who shared so generously her abiding love of flamenco and the secrets and surprises of old town Jerez, your adopted second home; to my aunt Maria who had the courage upon retirement to follow her heart's dream to go live in Spain at just the right time for me to meet up with you for those wonderful winter-lit days and nights in Madrid; to Joan Fleming, poet and fearless friend, also based in Madrid for a time, who read and re-read and encouraged me all the way; to kindred spirits in New Zealand, you know who you are, especially to Loveday Rose Why, for all the loving steps along the way, I thank you; and most of all, to family, to children now grown, and to Andi, who now knows why, I thank you. It is done.

www.ingramcontent.com/pod-product-compliance
Lightning Source LLC
Chambersburg PA
CBHW060947170426
43201CB00023B/2416